Original title:
Rings of Reflection

Copyright © 2025 Creative Arts Management OÜ
All rights reserved.

Author: Victor Mercer
ISBN HARDBACK: 978-1-80586-176-8
ISBN PAPERBACK: 978-1-80586-648-0

## Within the Glass

A clumsy cat, with grace it struts,
Leaping high, it slips and cuts.
It's not the floor, it's the air,
That catches whiskers in mid-flare.

Reflections laugh, as tail whips round,
The kitty's pride, dashed to the ground.
A dance with fate, what a sight,
In bouncing glass, it takes flight.

## **Refined Reverberations**

A pig in pearls, oh what a show,
Struts through the mud, with quite a glow.
Each step it takes, a squelchy sound,
Elegance lost, as splatters abound.

With every oink, a resounding cheer,
Refined, yet messy, oh dear, oh dear!
A truffle dream gone a tad awry,
In muddy splendor, it waves goodbye.

## Echoing Footsteps

A sock on the floor, just couldn't wait,
To jump in the laundry, it rode its fate.
Its partner's missing, oh what a shame,
An echoing dance, in a fashion game.

With every stumble and awkward toe,
It squeaks along, putting on a show.
A single sock's plight, brings laughter anew,
In the spin cycle, who knew it flew?

## The Radius of Dreams

A donut dreams of being a star,
Rolling through life, it travels far.
With frosting thick, and sprinkles bright,
It twirls around, a sugary sight.

But where's the hole? It wonders still,
Am I incomplete, against my will?
In the roundabout of tasty tales,
The donut giggles, as sweetness prevails.

## **Surfaces Beneath**

In pools of water, fish wear frowns,
They think they're clowns in shiny gowns.
The ducks all quack in silly beats,
While jumping frogs perform their feats.

A cat looks grand with whiskers wide,
Sees itself and puffs with pride.
The funhouse mirror's now a friend,
Where every twist ensures the blend.

### **Reflective Currents**

The river laughs, it swirls and spins,
While fish play tag with shiny fins.
A turtle grins, it strikes a pose,
In underwater fashion shows, who knows?

Each ripple sings a silly tune,
As frogs join in, loud as a loon.
Reflections wave with goofy glee,
Creating smiles for you and me.

## The Essence of Echoes

A voice calls back from down the hill,
It sounds like laughter, what a thrill!
The breeze replies with cheeky tones,
Like silly gnomes with rattling bones.

In caves, the echoes play their tricks,
Bouncing back with playful licks.
Each shout returns with such delight,
A giggling chorus late at night.

**The Carousel of Thoughts**

Round and round, ideas spin,
Like dizzy ducks in a whimsical din.
A thought pops up, it takes the lead,
While others chase like eager seeds.

Sometimes a concept trips and falls,
Creates a ruckus with silly calls.
In this wild ride, we share a laugh,
As thoughts collide in a happy craft.

## Ripples in Stillness

In a pond where ducks play,
My thoughts do a ballet.
Frogs in tuxedos leap high,
As I ponder the pizza pie.

The water swirls with delight,
As bubbles take flight.
A fish winks with glee,
I wonder if it can see me.

## **Encircling Thoughts**

Around and around I go,
Like a hamster without a show.
My ideas race, they collide,
In a tiny wheel, I can't hide.

Thoughts are like sushi rolls,
Some are funny, some are goals.
I chop and I mix with zest,
But the wasabi's a guest!

## Petals of Perspective

Daisies dance in a line,
Swaying to the tunes of wine.
Each petal tells a tale,
One's about a snail in a sail.

Butterflies flutter in pairs,
Wearing tiny flamboyant airs.
One whispers, 'Let's take a break,'
While the other insists on cake.

## Orbits of Understanding

Planets spin with a cheeky grin,
As stars throw a party again.
Gravity's playing hide and seek,
And the moon just loves to sneak.

Comets wave as they zoom by,
While aliens all say, 'Oh my!'
With laughter echoing far and wide,
They play tag on the cosmic ride.

## **Echoes in the Glass**

A mirror once told me a joke,
It laughed and said, 'You're a bloke!'
I winked and I smiled,
It giggled, beguiled.

Reflections that dance, oh so spry,
The light plays hide and seek, oh my!
I made a funny face,
And the glass lost its grace.

With echoes that twist and align,
I cracked up, it felt so divine.
The room sang with cheer,
As jokes came near.

## Cycles of Light

A lamp on the table went bright,
Claiming, 'I'm more fun at night!'
I told it to chill,
It flickered, then thrilled.

The sun popped in, what a sight!
'Your glow is a pale, poor light!'
The moon chuckled low,
'That's one heck of a show!'

Shadows danced in the room,
Adding a touch of gloom.
But laughter lived here,
As we all drew near.

## Fragments of Serenity

In a moment of calm, I declared,
'Life's quirks are beyond compared!'
A butterfly snickered,
As my plans all flickered.

The breeze got a kick out of jokes,
While teasing the nearby folks.
It whispered around,
Making laughter abound.

Underneath all the calm and the peace,
The giggles seemed never to cease.
In fragments we'd find,
The laughter unconfined.

**Circles of Contemplation**

Sitting in circles, we ponder,
On thoughts that are spicy as thunder.
A lightbulb went dim,
While I laughed at a whim!

We drew silly doodles with glee,
Contemplating what could not be.
Then one fellow said,
'Let's draw on our heads!'

The moments spun round, oh what fun,
Like clowns on a whim, we did run.
Through laughter and haste,
Life's circles embraced.

## Haloes of Insight

Oh look, a cloud, it says I'm wise,
I question that, as it twists and flies.
The sun above is laughing loud,
While shadows dance, a cheerful crowd.

A mirror's telling tales absurd,
It claims to speak without a word.
I nod and grin at its wry wit,
The wisdom's there, yet I must split.

## **Threads of Illumination**

A candle flickers, sneezes bright,
It spreads the cheer—what a delight!
Yet whispers low, it's just a flame,
But hey, it's still part of the game!

A flash of thought, it weaves my day,
Sewing laughter in a silly way.
With twinkling glints, my mind takes flight,
Each bright idea's a comic sight.

## Concentric Journeys

I took a trip to nowhere fast,
We circled once, then again we passed.
The GPS said, "Make a turn!"
I laughed aloud, it's just a burn!

In circles round, we spend our time,
What's next, a jigsaw, or a rhyme?
With each misstep, we find a way,
To giggle through the bloopers' play.

## Enigmas of the Heart

My heart once sighed, but then it spun,
With riddles wrapped, it thought it'd run.
A poke, a prod, it's playing coy,
A game of hide and seek—oh Joy!

I asked it straight, but got a wink,
This mystery loves a playful link.
With every twist, we trip and fall,
The dance of love is quite a ball!

**Shaded Silhouettes**

In the park, where shadows dance,
Squirrels mock with a sideways glance.
Lamps lean slightly, all askew,
The light just can't keep up with you.

A dog in shades, quite the sight,
Chasing rainbows, oh what a fright!
Cats in top hats appear from nowhere,
Sharing secrets in the cool night air.

## The Confluence of Echoes

In the canyon, echoes play,
Laughing back what we say.
'Yo, do we sound like that?' you cry,
The walls just wink and wave goodbye.

We mimic birds and even frogs,
Our voices turn to silly clogs.
The mountains chuckle, join the spree,
As all around, we shout with glee.

## **Whorls of Remembrance**

Spinning in the attic's fog,
Finding childhood's treasured log.
A stuffed bear wearing goofy shoes,
His name, it seems, is Captain Snooze.

Photographs warped by time's embrace,
Showing dance moves, a clumsy race.
Grandma's sweater, oh what a crime,
It looked better - just at one time!

## The Arc of Thought

With each idea that takes a flight,
My brain does somersaults – what a sight!
A circle here, a triangle there,
Thoughts flip-flop like they're at a fair.

A carousel of hopes now spins,
Around and round, where do we begin?
Laughter bubbles, ideas spark,
In the chaos, we find our mark.

## Circular Echoes

In a world where donuts reign,
I often lose my train of thought.
Chasing crumbs, I feel the strain,
This sugar rush cannot be bought.

Every bite takes me on a trip,
Round and round, like a merry-goat.
Sticky fingers make me slip,
Oh, how I love this calorie boat!

A pizza pie may steal the show,
But I'm in love with a round cake.
Fools like me, we just don't know,
That rolling dough is no mistake!

Yet here I am, with sprinkles bright,
Counting calories, what a fight!
While all the shapes just spin and twirl,
I laugh and taste my donut world.

## Undulating Insights

Life's a wave, a bouncy ball,
It lifts you high then lets you drop.
You know you'll rise; you're having a ball,
Just hope the floor isn't made of slop!

Each bounce and jiggle makes me giggle,
Like wobbly jelly on a paper plate.
Trying to balance, my feet do wiggle,
At times like these, I just can't wait!

Thoughts roll in like a beachside tide,
Some are pearls, some are just sand.
I'll ride the waves, take 'em in stride,
With laughter leading, life's just grand!

So, here's to ups, and downs, and flips,
Let's laugh at life's undying quirks.
When the wave retreats, we'll play like chips,
Bouncing back with all the perks!

## The Spiral of Being

Twists and turns are quite absurd,
Like a noodle tossed with glee.
Life's a roller coaster, haven't you heard?
Clinging tight to my cup of tea!

Round and round, we do a dance,
Like squirrels chasing their own tails.
Every step, a glorious chance,
To hop along where laughter sails.

The world's a circus, full of gags,
With mimes and clowns, in vibrant hues.
Just when you think you've got the tags,
Life throws you an unexpected bruise!

So let's embrace this winding path,
With silly hats and quirky shoes.
For in the maelstrom of life's math,
Laughter's the only way to choose!

## **Glimmering Memories**

In my attic lies a box of cheer,
With photos that make me snicker.
There's Uncle Bob, who spilled his beer,
In grandma's hat, what a wild flicker!

Each snapshot glows like glittering lights,
Times when we danced on kitchen floors.
With tangled hair and silly tights,
We laughed till we fell between the doors.

Remember that time a cake exploded?
Frosting swirled like a happy storm.
Laughter erupted, and chaos loaded,
Our memories, a bright, silly swarm!

So here's to moments that make us beam,
To glimmering times we won't outlive.
With each fond laugh, we'll weave a dream,
In our hearts, the joy will always give!

## Shadows of the Past

I tripped on my past, oh what a sight,
My socks were mismatched, so wrong, yet so bright.
A dance with my youth, I stumbled on air,
As nostalgia giggled, my thoughts laid bare.

The times that I wore such outrageous flair,
Platform shoes towering, I hadn't a care.
A record that skipped, much like my old brain,
Yet laughter and chaos revisit again.

Those styles that once dazzled, now cause some dread,
Like bell-bottom jeans that could swallow your head.
In the shuffle of memories, joy and a tease,
Blurred lines of history bring back the cheese.

So here's to the moments we can't quite forget,
With shadows that dance in a whimsical duet.
Though wisdom may grow, I'll keep that kid near,
For shadows of past bring both laughter and cheer.

## Enchanted Circles

In a world of delight, where oddities spin,
Where squirrels wear top hats, let the fun begin.
I chased a round shape with pockets of glee,
Hoping to find what the magic could be.

With cupcakes that talk and trees that can sing,
I stumbled upon unexpected strange things.
A circle of friends wore mismatched bow ties,
As we laughed at our socks that brought joyful cries.

Bubbles that burst into fits of pure laughter,
In enchanted circles, I found the key after.
A pie fight ensued, then we danced on the green,
In this merry domain, where joy's evergreen.

So twirl in the magic, let cynics be glum,
For circles of laughter are better than some.
With whimsy as currency, let's savor the spree,
In enchanted dimensions, we're young and carefree!

## Drifting in the Round

A donut-shaped dream where giggles collide,
As round shapes roll past me, I smile wide-eyed.
The cat stole my sandwich, it bounced in delight,
With visions of food fights that tickle the night.

With puddles of joy, I hop skip and twirl,
While my hat takes a dive, causing chaos to swirl.
I'm drifting, I'm spinning, in circles I play,
As marshmallows giggle and dance through the fray.

Oh, the whimsy of life as we float in our fun,
While bananas parade under rays of the sun.
In this roundabout madness, there's no place for frowns,
Just joyful distractions and upside-down towns.

So let's drift together on laughter's sweet tide,
With silliness guiding wherever we glide.
For in this wild whirlpool of joy found in sound,
We cherish our wanderings, drifting around!

## **The Orbit of Memories**

A spaceship of laughter zooms past my head,
With aliens wearing pajamas instead.
We orbit around all our fanciful dreams,
Spinning tales of laughter that sparkle like beams.

The planets are cookies, the stars are fireworks,
As I tumble through time where the silly still works.
In this galaxy, memories float and collide,
Tickling my heart with each joyous ride.

When days seem monotonous, take off your frown,
And launch into orbit, let go of the crown.
For the laughter you gather is priceless, you see,
As we spin through our stories so wild and free.

So here's to the orbits of chuckles and cheer,
Where memories linger, forever sincere.
In this universe vast where the funny prevails,
We sail on the laughter like ships with bright sails.

## Waves of Introspection

Water splashes on my feet,
The fish all swimming neat.
I ponder life's crazy dance,
Should I wear that silly pants?

Seagulls swoop and make a sound,
Chasing their snacks all around.
I wonder if they have plans,
Or just snatch fries from my hands?

Little crabs scuttle fast,
A race that seems to last.
I join in like I'm a pro,
Turn the sand into my show!

Under the sun, I laugh and play,
Chasing shadows all day.
With each wave that comes to shore,
I find myself wanting more!

**The Dance of Shadows**

Beneath the streetlamp's glow,
My shadow starts to flow.
It jiggles, wobbles with cheer,
Saying, "Dance! Come over here!"

The cats just stare in a line,
Watching my shadow divine.
They think I'm losing my mind,
But I'm just seeking some kind!

A raccoon joins the fiasco,
And starts a two-step tango.
Together we spin and groove,
In this wild nighttime move.

With laughter echoing loud,
We become a silly crowd.
Who knew shadows could have fun?
Join this bizarre evening run!

**Concentric Dreams**

In circles, I draw my plans,
Of pies and funny cans.
Round and round, my thoughts concede,
That life is more than just a seed.

I dream of donuts, warm and sweet,
Imagining each tasty treat.
But as I eat, I laugh to see,
The calories don't let me be!

Hula hoops I toss and play,
With every twist, I must obey.
Round and round, I go quite stark,
Making dial-up sounds in the park!

Carnival rides spin me around,
Yet upside down, joy is found.
In every twirl, what's the scheme?
Life's a double scoop ice cream!

**Fragments of Infinity**

In a world of bits and bobs,
I collect the funny odds.
A sock without its mate,
Is just a little less great!

Lego bricks and jelly jars,
Crafting dreams that reach the stars.
Chaos creates its own tune,
Building castles, whistling a rune.

The paradox of things that break,
A spoon that laughs, a silly quack.
Dance with the items that misplace,
Each a fragment in this space.

As I ponder all these finds,
A giggle slips, and truth unwinds.
For every piece that doesn't fit,
Is part of this great cosmic skit!

## Veils of Clarity

Through curtains of mist, I make my way,
Wearing socks that clash—what do they say?
Buffoons in the fog, tripping on clues,
Chasing my thoughts like old, runaway shoes.

A peek through the haze, what do I see?
A cat in a hat, sipping tea with me!
I crack a joke to the lamp on my desk,
It dims its bright light—was my humor too grotesque?

Blurry reflections dance on the wall,
A shadow, a giggle—a rise and a fall.
Life's just a circus, but hey, that's alright,
I juggle my worries till I vanish from sight.

So here's to the fog that wraps us in jest,
In veils of confusion, we give it our best.
We kayaked through nonsense, no maps in our hand,
In laughter, we found joy—our wobbly stand.

## **Spiral Embraces**

Round and around, we chase silly tales,
A hamster on wheels, the crowd just aails.
With each little twirl, we bring on the cheer,
Unexpected embraces, and snacks... oh my dear!

Whirling like dinner plates, who dropped their fries?
A cat with a crown, and oh, how she pries!
In spirals of laughter, we tumble and spin,
Like socks in the dryer, where chaos begins.

The dance of confusion, we waltz through the night,
Stumbling on punchlines, what gave us this fright?
Yet giggles abound, like candy in jars,
We bask in the light of a hundred funny stars.

So guide your feet gently on this dizzying track,
In circles of humor, there's nothing we lack.
As we spiral on down, let's not lose our shoes,
With hearts intertwined, we'll shake off the blues.

## Cascades of Emotion

A waterfall of giggles spills over my head,
With splashes of joy, I gather my bread.
In layers of puns, I dive in the flow,
Life's so absurd, let's see how far we go.

From chuckles to snorts, the river runs wild,
I float on a raft made of mischief and mild.
Each wave, a new jest that cascades and breaks,
We ride the emotions—oh, look, it quakes!

Sailing through sighs, like ducks on the pond,
As we leap over quips, of which we are fond.
With bubbles of laughter, the spray fills the air,
A fountain of fun—just look at my hair!

So dive in, dear friend, put worries aside,
In cascades of humor, let's take a wild ride.
With laughter as our guide, the current will steer,
What fun is the journey if we aren't sincere?

## Lighthouses of the Mind

In the fog of my thoughts, I see a bright flash,
A lighthouse of humor, through waves, it will clash.
Guiding those lost, with a wink and a smile,
Chasing down punchlines, let's linger a while.

The beacon can wobble, it might even spin,
As thoughts light the way, where to begin?
With quirks and odd tales, we forge our own path,
Navigating laughter, escaping the wrath.

Each wave crashes down, but we dance through the night,
With shadows of whimsy, we revel in light.
Mismatched socks guide us, how silly they seem,
In this lighthouse of nonsense, we're living the dream.

So raise up a toast to the quirks we embrace,
To the lighthouses bright that lead us with grace.
For through all the twists, with laughter entwined,
We find our true treasures in the depths of the mind.

## **The Continuum of Heartbeats**

There once was a heart full of cheer,
It beat out a tune for all near.
With each funky thump,
It jumped like a lump,
Making folks giggle and sneer.

When it felt a little shy,
It would hide, oh my my!
But then out it sprang,
With a loud, goofy clang,
Leaving friends to wonder why.

At parties, it danced with delight,
A bump here, a thump there, what a sight!
So folks did agree,
That this heart, you see,
Made every dull moment feel bright.

And while other hearts throbbed straight,
This one found humor in fate.
With a giggle or two,
It became quite the crew,
Teaching laughter is never too late.

## **Phases of the Soul**

Once a soul had a bumbling phase,
It tripped through the fog in a daze.
But it stumbled with style,
And wore a big smile,
As life sparked its silly malaise.

In a jump and a twist, it would whir,
Like a confused little bird with a blur.
Though it fell on its face,
It adorned every space,
With joy like a bright, goofy spur.

Through chuckles and giggles, it learned,
That each twist turned into a fern.
With every mishap,
Came a hearty clap,
As the funny life lessons were earned.

Oh, the phases it wore made it bright,
Each one a comedic delight!
So the soul would just grin,
With each tumble and spin,
And dance into the full moonlight.

## Luminescent Visions

In a land where the bright lights collide,
A vision would think, then would glide.
It whispered out dreams,
With giggles and beams,
As joy became its favorite ride.

With winks from the stars all around,
This vision found playtime abound.
It twirled in the air,
With flair made to spare,
Creating laughter from every sound.

Each flicker was filled with a jest,
Making merry, it felt like the best.
In a burst of shine,
It made funny lines,
Turning gloom into pure, silly zest.

So if you can catch a glimpse bright,
Of visions that twinkle at night,
Just dance and let go,
Join the spirit's flow,
And fill life with laughter and light.

## The Tidal Circle

In the waves of a laugh, there's a spin,
A circular joy that breaks in.
With each crest and each fall,
It beckons us all,
To jump in, let the humor begin!

The tides would rise high, then would sway,
As giggles rolled in like a bay.
They tickled our toes,
In a splash, off it goes,
Leaving joy in its frothy ballet.

With the moon giving signals to play,
The water would dance, then relay.
As each wave would crash,
We'd tumble and splash,
Laughing louder with each bright display.

So why not just let yourself flow,
In a current of laughter and glow?
In this tidal embrace,
Find your funny place,
And ride every wave, nice and slow.

## **Whispers on Water**

A pebble plops, oh what a splash,
Frogs leap high, then belly crash.
Ducklings dance, their feet so swift,
With every ripple, they give a lift.

Bubbles giggle as they rise,
Fish wear sneaky, fishy ties.
The wind winks, the trees do sway,
Nature's jokes, come out to play.

A turtle chuckles, slow and wise,
He takes a nap beneath the skies.
Sunbeams tickle, waves go 'whoosh',
A playful splash, yet another swoosh!

So let the water tell its tale,
Of every laugh and every fail.
For in its depths, we find the cheer,
A world where giggles float right here.

**Luminous Layers**

In the attic, dust bunnies zoom,
They throw a party in the gloom.
Light chases shadows, what a game!
Each corner whispers a funny name.

Old photographs dance with glee,
A blurry face, oh that's just me!
Time wears layers like a coat,
A hodgepodge of quirks, a silly note.

The clock strikes twelve with a loud tick,
Surprised, the cat does a backflip.
Candles wobble, trying to sing,
Each flicker joins in on the fling.

Memories twirl, they take a chance,
In luminous layers, they prance.
A scrapbook of laughter, bright and bold,
In every page, a story told.

## **Mirrors of Time**

A puddle laughs, reflections fun,
It shows a rabbit on the run.
With floppy ears and twitching nose,
What else it hides, who truly knows?

A mirror winks, it loves the tease,
It shows off hairdos with the breeze.
One day a prince, the next a frog,
Life's silly dance in a swirling fog.

Old clocks tick-tock, echoing cheer,
As if they know, time's worth a beer.
Each tick a giggle, each tock a grin,
In the game of life, we all wear thin.

So hold that mirror, take a peek,
In the glass, it's laughter we seek.
For time's a jest, and oh what fun,
In dreams and giggles, we are all one.

## The Orb of Memory

An orb rolls in with a funny face,
It knows our secrets, our silly grace.
With a wink and a nod, it spins around,
Gathering stories lost and found.

It whispers tales of socks gone rogue,
Of dancing shoes, of an old gold brogue.
Each gleam reveals a moment bright,
A time for laughter, a song of light.

Friends and pranks all live inside,
The orb chuckles, takes us for a ride.
Through every giggle, every silly scheme,
Memories swirl like a daydream theme.

So let it roll, that orb of cheer,
Reminding us to hold family near.
For in its glow, we find our way,
With laughter echoing, come what may.

## **Harmonies in the Void**

In a world where thoughts do spin,
Echoes of laughter, let the fun begin.
Bubbles of joy float through the air,
Dancing in pairs without a care.

Chirpy birds gossip in a breeze,
Jokes fly high with the greatest of ease.
A cat wears a hat, oh what a sight,
Sipping on tea, feeling just right.

Mice play chess in the moon's soft glow,
Winning by chance, but who would know?
Stars giggle and wink, all in good jest,
In the void, humor really is best.

So grab your friends and let's all sing,
In this quirky realm where laughter is king.
We'll toast to the moments, silly and bright,
In every giggle, there's pure delight.

## Emblems of Wisdom

A wise old turtle wears specs so thick,
Arguing with a rock—oh what a trick!
Wisdom's not just in books, we see,
Sometimes it naps in a cup of tea.

A squirrel in slippers talks to a shoe,
"Life's too short for socks that are blue!"
Philosophers meet at the edge of a stream,
Debating the merits of ice cream.

With owls who hoot 'bout the meaning of fate,
And frogs in tuxedos who always are late.
They ponder and ponder, till night turns to dawn,
Proclaiming real wisdom lies in the yawn.

So let's tip our hats to the thoughts that amuse,
In this silly world, there's no need to choose.
For laughter and wisdom dance hand in hand,
In the quirkiest thoughts, we make our stand.

## Tides of Awareness

The moon whispers secrets to the sea,
While fish wear sunglasses and sip on green tea.
A crab plays the flute, oh what a sound!
Harmony's waving all around.

Seagulls debate on who flies the best,
While waves giggle softly, taking a rest.
Starfish exercise, stretching with flair,
Balancing dreams in the salty air.

Each ripple carries tales of the day,
Where jellyfish dance 'til they sway.
The ocean's a playground, let's all dive in,
With buoyant ideas and a cheeky grin.

So splash in the fun, let the tides take you high,
To shores of imagination where laughter won't die.
In the waves of awareness, we find our own way,
Embracing the silly, come what may!

**Shimmers of Tomorrow**

Dewdrops glisten on a silly snail,
Sliding down rainbows, leaving a trail.
With dreams made of candy and wishes of spry,
Tomorrow awaits with a wink in its eye.

Gummy bears bounce to a tune so sweet,
While lollipop trees sway to the beat.
A parade of marshmallows marches on by,
As chocolate rivers are flowing high.

Tomorrow's a canvas, bright and absurd,
Where pigeons write essays and are never deterred.
Silly inventions, like shoes that can sing,
Make the future a place for the wildest bling.

So grab your popcorn and sit down to see,
The shimmering moments await you and me.
With laughter, we'll carve out our own silly space,
In a tomorrow that's filled with joy and grace.

## Once Upon a Circlet

In a land where donuts reign,
Where sprinkles dance and giggle in vain,
A hero sought a circle so round,
To wear on his head, quite profound!

He tried a bagel, it slipped from sight,
A hula hoop? Too much for a bite!
At last, a loop of spaghetti so true,
Now he's the king of the noodle crew!

With praise from the pasta, laughter did swell,
His crown of carbs, no one could quell,
The jester of rings, he twirled with glee,
In his cheesy kingdom, he ruled with a spree!

Each circle he wore, like life's silly dance,
A noodle that twirls—what a fate, what a chance!
In laughter they roamed, his court so bizarre,
With a crown of linguine, they traveled afar!

## Fractal Memories

In a maze of thoughts, I stumbled around,
Saw a chicken dressed up, looking quite profound,
It clucked and it danced, in fractals it spun,
A memory of laughter—oh, what fun!

Reflective reflections, the mirrors would tease,
In every angle, a new joke would freeze,
A frog in a tux, at a fancy soirée,
I laughed till I cried—what a vibrant display!

The coffee cups chatted, each sip a delight,
They spilled their own stories, from day into night,
"Did you see that bird?" one cup said with flair,
"Feathered and tangled, it flew through the air!"

In the fractal of life, humor grows wide,
From each silly moment, we cannot hide,
So here's to the echoes of all that we share,
With a wink and a smile, let's dance through the air!

## The Harmony of Stillness

In a quiet little town, where whispers abound,
Sat a cat on a fence, that purred without sound,
With eyes like two saucers, it plotted a deed,
To nap in stillness, oh, what a sweet need!

The squirrels held a concert, complete with a show,
Each nut they performed, it stole quite the glow,
But our feline friend snored through the grand ball,
Missing the tune of the woodland's enthrall!

A butterfly fluttered, as grand as could be,
Dancing between branches, so wild and free,
Yet still in repose, the cat would remain,
In harmony cozy, where silence feels plain!

So let us embrace the quiet, the laugh,
In moments of stillness, we craft our own path,
For sometimes the best joys are found when we pause,
Like a sleepy-eyed cat, who just dreams of applause!

## Harmonies of Reflection

In a pond, a frog sings loud,
Croaks echo, draws quite a crowd.
A fish swims by with a silly grin,
Bubbles rise, let the fun begin!

Shadows dance in the bright moonlight,
A cat leaps out, gives quite a fright.
Chasing echoes, making a mess,
Who knew reflections could be such a jest?

Laughter rises, a magical sound,
Even the trees sway around.
With melody shared, all of a sudden,
The whole place feels like a giggling puddin'.

When puddles reflect, the jokes collide,
In splashes of water, cheer can't hide.
Unexpected fun in every glare,
In this shiny world, there's joy to share!

## The Convergence of Time

Tick-tock goes the silly clock,
Time slips by, a playful shock.
Seconds dance, some twirl in place,
While minutes goof with a funny face.

A squirrel scurries, but waits to freeze,
As time laughs hard, brings him to knees.
Round and round, the hands will play,
In this merry chase, they never stay.

Hiccups of moments crash and collide,
Time's a jester, can't ever hide.
Every tick can tickle your mind,
In a kaleidoscope, fun's intertwined!

So when you see the hourglass fall,
Smile wide as you trip and stall.
For in the chaos, joy you'll find,
Time's just the punchline, oh so kind!

## **Mirror of the Past**

In a funhouse, mirrors bend and weave,
Reflecting laughs that you can't believe.
A face that's wide, then oh so small,
A silly dance, can't help but fall!

Ghosts of memories wink and play,
Showing you things in a quirky way.
Mom's old shoes make you trip again,
While Grandpa's jokes just never end.

Through the glass, antics collide,
Every glance, brings giggles inside.
It's memory lane but a bit askew,
Where every laugh loops back to you!

So spin around, give it a whirl,
In this maze of fun, let laughter unfurl.
With every reflection, a chuckle's cast,
A joyful reminder of your funny past!

## Unending Spirals

Round and round, like a rollercoaster,
Life takes twists, a spirited toaster.
Up and down, with a whoop and a sway,
Every turn makes you giggle and play.

With spirals of candy, colors galore,
Each twisty path leads to laughter more.
Chasing your tail, what a sight to see,
In this topsy-turvy life with glee!

Falling like leaves that whirl in the air,
Spirals of fun, without a care.
Jumping through hoops that giggle and jest,
Life's just a merry-go-round at its best!

So twirl and twist, embrace the delight,
With every cycle, shine so bright.
For in this spiraled, joyful ride,
Funny moments become a wild slide!

## The Loop of Memories

In the attic, I found my old bike,
With two flat tires and a bell that won't strike.
I pedaled through years of my youthful glee,
Chasing squirrels, or was it just me?

Those moments loop like a skipping song,
Where I thought I was right, but was wrong all along.
With stories so wild, they'd give you a fit,
Like that time I danced and fell in my split.

Grandma's stories of boys on the run,
And I laughed till I cried, oh, wasn't that fun?
Her wig was a hat flying high in the air,
And I still can't recall why I even cared.

So let's toast to the echoes of laughter and play,
To moments that loop like a long, crazy ballet.
Memories dance, spin round and round,
Making each day a joy that I've found.

## **Silvered Surfaces**

On a spoon, I saw my reflection today,
With crookèd smile, who knew I could sway?
I winked at myself, gave a playful cheer,
But the biscuit in hand stole the whole scene, dear!

In the kettle, my face took a bubbly shape,
With hair like a bird's nest, escape!
It whistled a tune, I couldn't help but dance,
While pouring my tea, talking to my chance.

The cat watched me stumble, the kettle would sigh,
As I tripped on a rug, oh my, oh my!
Just how many reflections can one kitchen hold?
In this funny old life, I'm a sight to behold!

So here's to the silvered, polished tales,
That twist and that turn like whimsical gales.
With laughter our only guiding light,
We sip at life's tea, oh what a delight!

## **Cycles of Light**

The sun came up with a wink and a grin,
As I tripped on my shoelaces, again and again.
Each ray teased my brain with a new silly thought,
While I fumbled for coffee, can't find what I sought!

I spun in circles, the shadows did taunt,
Like a spotlight on me when I'm in the front.
I knocked over the plants, they won't hold a grudge,
But I swear they laughed, oh how they judge!

Reflecting on blunders, oh what a mix,
Each day is a joke, we're all part of the fix.
Like kids playing tag with a mischievous sun,
We chase after visions, thinking we won!

So let's twirl through the oops and the cheers,
With cycles of laughter that ring in our ears.
For every bright moment that catches our sight,
Remember we're here for a dance in the light!

## Encircling Thoughts

Round and round my brain goes today,
Chasing thoughts like cats that decide to play.
They hide in the corners, they dance on the shelf,
When you search for wisdom, it just laughs at itself.

I thought of a poem, then lost it at sea,
It was riding a wave, giggling, you see.
Where did it go? Perhaps it took flight,
On the back of a bird that thinks it's all right.

So here I am pondering, what to do next,
When a thought simply slips, it leaves me perplexed.
Like a boomerang lost in the depths of a swing,
It circles back home, but I can't find a thing!

So let's dance on the loops of our silly old fears,
And swirl with the joy that we find through the years.
For every thought lost is a giggle to share,
In the encircling madness, there's love everywhere!

## Reflections of the Heart

In the pond, a frog jumps high,
It sees its face, thinks it's a spy.
With bulging eyes and warty skin,
It plots a heist, ready to win.

A cat strolls by, with swagger so bold,
It sees itself, feels a bit sold.
Puffed-up tail, a royal decree,
"I'm the best, just wait and see!"

The dog joins in, with a sideways glance,
Gives a bark and thinks it's a dance.
Wagging its tail, full of clever tricks,
Reflecting that it's not just for kicks.

In the end, with a splash and a cheer,
They laugh at their faces, both far and near.
Wobbling thoughts in the water so sweet,
Who knew reflections could be such a treat?

## The Looking Glass Path

Through the mirror, I sneak a peek,
What's that? A smile? A cheek to cheek!
My hair's a mess, my shirt's inside out,
This path of hilarity leaves no doubt.

A squirrel dressed like a pop star in style,
Stops and winks with a nutty smile.
It twirls around, showing off its moves,
In this wacky world, everyone grooves.

A rabbit hops, wearing big red shoes,
It sings a tune that sounds like blues.
Just then a turtle, all slow and wise,
Checks its reflection, with squinty eyes.

Dancing shadows on the cobblestones clear,
Echoes of laughter fill the air near.
In this mirrored path, where nonsense reigns,
Fun and folly are our silly chains.

**Constellations of Mind**

Gazing up at the starry night,
A potato floats, what a funny sight!
With a twinkle here, and a giggle there,
The moon chuckles, gives me a stare.

Venus winks, wearing a silly hat,
While Mars plays tag with an old tired cat.
Jupiter's belly shakes with laughter,
While Saturn spins tales of diet disaster.

In this grand scheme of celestial ways,
Each planet shines in whimsical plays.
"Hey, Earth!" they shout, "What's your new scheme?"
I chuckle and say, "Just living the dream!"

As comets dash by with a bright little trail,
The cosmos chuckles, setting the sail.
For in this universe of laughter and light,
Every thought sparkles, shines through the night!

## **Glacial Reflections**

On a glacier, where the penguins prance,
They slide on ice, engaging in dance.
Waddling and flapping, a mischievous bunch,
Thinking they can start the coolest lunch.

An old polar bear, with a frosty grin,
Looks at his reflection, and lets out a din.
"I'm the king of this ice, made of delight!"
He nibbles on fish, a slippery bite.

The seals bark out chorus, a funny tune,
As the moon watches with a quizzical swoon.
In this frosty realm, where giggles are rare,
All creatures unite in cold, funny flair.

Through glacial mirrors, laughter does sway,
Creating memories in a chilly play.
For in the domain of frozen terrain,
Even the ice smiles, shedding a stain.

## **Circular Journeys**

Round and round in circles we go,
Chasing our tails, oh what a show.
The dog in the yard joins the dance,
Do we ever stop to take a glance?

Around the sun, we spin with glee,
Dodging flying pies, oh how can it be?
A journey that owns no single path,
Just laughter and joy, and a bit of math.

Wobbly trips to find what we seek,
Falling into puddles, oh how unique!
With every step, a new twist and turn,
Lessons of life – oh, when will we learn?

So here we spin, like tops on a floor,
With every giggle, we want more and more.
In circles we travel, no need to fret,
On this funny journey, there's no regret!

## The Veil of Reflection

I looked in the mirror, what did I see?
A face full of laughter staring back at me.
With toothpaste smudges and a wild hairdo,
Is that truly me, or a funhouse view?

A veil of giggles, a wall of cheer,
Echoes of laughter fill the air near.
Each glance reveals a new silly pose,
A dance of the goofy, in jigs and throws.

Reflections amuse in the silliest way,
Like a clown's nose on a sunny day.
We might get serious, but not for long,
Laughter's the anthem, our favorite song.

Behind the glass, we share a wink,
Amusing antics that make us think.
So here's to the fun, the silly, the bright,
Let's flip the switch and dance in delight!

## Polished Edges

Shiny and bright, with edges so neat,
Each step I take feels like a treat.
I tripped on my shoes; they gleam like the sun,
Laughing feels good when it's all said and done.

Polished to perfection, like a brand new toy,
But watch where you step or you might lose your joy.
With slippery soles and a skip in my stride,
Every smooth surface becomes the ride.

In a world full of mirrors, I wave and I twirl,
But flaunting my fancy is such a swirl.
Every reflection brings a fresh surprise,
Here's to the shine that brightens our eyes!

So let's laugh at the missteps, embrace the shine,
In this swirling dance, everything's fine.
We polish our edges, but not just for show,
In the brightness of laughter, we all want to grow!

## Timeless Edges

Time is a joker, with tricks up its sleeve,
It jests and it jumbles, oh it's hard to believe.
With a tick-tock tangle, the clock starts to tease,
Can time really dance? Oh, do it with ease!

In a timeless world, we giggle and spin,
Past all the boundaries, the fun's about to begin.
So many mischiefs in a wink of an eye,
It's a laugh-a-minute as moments fly by.

Edges blur, yet the smile stays bright,
In a dance of the days and a twirl through the night.
When we trip on our feet, let's burst out in cheer,
For every odd moment, new joy will appear!

So here's to the laughter, to time's silly games,
To tickles and giggles, oh, how it inflames!
With timeless adventures that never grow old,
Let's cherish the stories that we dare to unfold!

## The Flow of Reflections

In the mirror, I make a face,
A questionable grin, oh what a place!
My reflection's doing a silly dance,
I giggle out loud—what a strange romance!

Water splashes as ducks waddle by,
Quacking their jokes, oh how they fly!
I can't keep up, they're too quick for me,
Splashing in puddles, pure jubilee!

When I jump in, I create a ripple,
The ducks stop laughing; oh, what a tipple!
My hair's a mess, feathers in the fray,
In this kooky pool, I'm here to stay!

So let's toast to the chaos we see,
In the world of the wobbly and utterly free!
With each gleam and giggle, the fun's not done,
Just another day—oh what a pun!

## **Holographic Moments**

In a world made of light and snickers,
Each pixel whispers, oh how it flickers!
I think I saw my shoe in 3D,
It waved goodbye—where could it be?

Lost in a realm of floating dreams,
Where jellybeans rain and nothing's as it seems.
My thoughts are deflated like a sad balloon,
Wobbling around like a silly cartoon!

I asked a shadow, 'What's the joke?'
It shrugged its shoulders, the poor bloke!
I laughed so hard, I forgot my name,
In this hologram, it's all just a game!

So here's to moments where nonsense rules,
In a zany world filled with fun-loving fools!
Each laugh, a spark, igniting the night,
In this crazy realm, we shine so bright!

## **Cascade of Thoughts**

Thoughts tumble down like a waterfall,
Bouncing on rocks, oh what a brawl!
An idea slips, and I start to giggle,
Like a bad pun or a silly wiggle!

I chased a daydream, it ran so fast,
Tripped on my shoelace, fell at last!
With my head in the clouds and feet on the ground,
I pondered out loud while my socks were unbound!

The squirrels had a rave, tails a-flutter,
Dancing 'round nuts, in a nutty clutter!
I joined the frenzy, a whimsical sight,
Twirled 'round the tree till I took flight!

So let these cascades bring joy to the day,
Where thoughts twirl and muddle, and giggles play!
In this charming chaos, let's twine and swirl,
A jolly embrace, in this whimsical whirl!

## The Conduit of Clarity

Through the fog of laughter, I peer with glee,
Searching for answers, where could they be?
I stumbled on wisdom, tucked behind a chair,
It winked at me, without a care!

A potato spoke, in clear, crisp tones,
"Life's like a salad, with wobbly bones!"
I pondered its words, while munching a fry,
This conduit to clarity had me in a tie!

The cat chimed in, with a wise, soft meow,
"Just seek the sillies, they'll show you how!"
Together we giggled, a trio absurd,
In this realm of clarity, every word's heard!

So raise up a toast, to nonsense and cheer,
In this quirky journey, let's all steer clear!
With humor as our guide, and laughter as key,
In this joyous chaos, forever we'll be!

## **Roundabout Journeys**

Around we go, a spin so nice,
Chasing our tails, not once but thrice.
Lost in the circle, we laugh and shout,
Is this the start or just the route?

Bumpy paths and honking cars,
GPS broken, chasing stars.
Every wrong turn feels like a jest,
Who knew getting lost could be the best?

The road gets twisty; we follow the fun,
A game of hide and seek on the run.
With every loop, a story we share,
Roundabouts love a band of the rare.

So here's to the merry-go-round of life,
With laughter and joy, forgetting the strife.
Round and round, let's keep the cheer,
On this journey, there's nothing to fear!

## **The Halo of Moments**

A bright little circle floats in the air,
Catching the giggles; do you want to share?
Moments like bubbles, gleaming and round,
When they pop with laughter, joy's truly found.

In a world of chaos, they waltz through time,
Each one a jest, each moment a rhyme.
A halo of giggles flies high overhead,
Thank goodness we've got our funny bone fed!

Smiling at blunders, we dance and we sway,
Life's silly moments, come join the ballet!
Round moonlit nights, the silliness glows,
A halo of laughter wherever it goes.

So let's twirl and wobble, hold tight to the glee,
The joy of this circle is wild and carefree.
With friends all around, we can't lose our way,
In this circle of moments, forever we'll play!

## **Threads of Reflection**

Weaving through laughter, we spin and we glide,
With threads of our quirks tightly tied inside.
Reflecting on mishaps like shining a light,
Every tumble a treasure, each laugh takes flight.

Silly shenanigans stitched into our seams,
Tangled in joy, we chase after dreams.
With every loose thread comes a story to tell,
Of mishaps and mix-ups that unravel so well.

A fabric of friendship as vibrant as day,
The patterns of laughter never fade away.
In this quilt of mirth, we cover the ground,
Every thread a giggle, a joy that we've found.

So come share your tales, let's weave them anew,
In this tapestry bright, there's a space for you.
With each stitch of fun, we climb to great heights,
In threads of reflection, the world feels just right!

## **Refracted Souls**

Through prisms of laughter, our souls twist and turn,
Bending the light, where the chuckles we earn.
We shimmer and shine in the silliest way,
Like rainbows of joy chasing clouds far away.

With every snap of the light, we disperse,
Creating a spectrum of giggles, what's worse?
Finding that humor in shadows and sun,
Refracted and bent, we laugh just for fun.

Our spirits collide in a hilarious dance,
Each glance is a spark, a whimsical chance.
In the laughter's embrace, we find our true home,
A carnival of colors that helps us to roam.

So let's twirl in the light, let our weirdness unfold,
With refracted souls, our stories retold.
In this vivid diversion, together we play,
In the prism of joy, we'll forever stay!

## Labyrinths of Self.

In the mirror, I see my face,
A dance party in a tiny space.
My hair does a jig, my nose takes flight,
Who knew I was a clown at night?

I ponder my life, in circles I roam,
Do I take the bus, or just walk home?
With socks mismatched, a fashion faux pas,
Is it me, or is it just the way things are?

With every turn, I lose my track,
Lost among thoughts, but I won't look back.
Like a spaghetti twist on a dinner plate,
Self-discovery, oh, it can wait!

Inside my head, there's a party on loop,
A conga line formed by a mismatched troupe.
Balancing woes, with a laugh and a scream,
In this merry maze, life's just a dream.

## Echoes in the Water

A splash! A giggle, a funny face,
The ducks applaud in their quacking grace.
I see myself in waves so bright,
Did I just lose a splash fight tonight?

Canoeing in circles, like a fish out of stew,
Paddling backwards, who knew I could do?
My oar goes left, but I steer too right,
I make ducks laugh, it's quite the sight.

Water reflections whisper a prank,
Is that my hair, or some seaweed flank?
I wave at my twin, she waves back with cheer,
Hello, mirror me, we're quite the pair here!

Drifting in ripples, no worries in sight,
Just laughing at nothing, it's sheer delight.
Together we float, with echoes so grand,
Life's just a joke, go ahead, take a stand.

## Circular Whispers

In circles we twirl, like tops on the floor,
Chasing our tails, oh, what's in store?
I step on my shoelace, I trip, I take flight,
Rolling like dough, what a silly sight.

Whispers of giggles drift through the air,
Conversations with walls, it's only fair.
They give solid advice, when I'm feeling blue,
"Just flip your hair, it'll all feel new!"

It's a roundabout way to find some peace,
With humor and jest, let the laughter increase.
Fools in a circus, we juggle our wits,
In the dance of dumb, there's no need for splits.

As life goes around, we join hands and spin,
Making merry-go-rounds, free of chagrin.
Let's roll in silliness, let laughter unfurl,
In circles, my friend, we can conquer the whirl.

## Reflections in the Stillness

In the calm of the pond, I see my good side,
A swan looks back; we're quite a wide ride.
With a peck and a bounce, we make quite the pair,
Just two silly fools with feathers to spare.

With thoughts like bubbles, I giggle and float,
Am I a chicken in another life's coat?
Clucks and laughs, I tiptoe the line,
Life's a grand joke, with laughter divine.

Staring at stillness, the fish wave hello,
They swim in circles, in bubbles they glow.
Oh, to dive deep in this glamorous life,
The absurdity bright, despite the small strife.

In reflections of quiet, I twirl and I sway,
With a wink at the cosmos, I'm here to play.
In stillness, I find all my giggles and glee,
A laugh at the world and the world laughs with me.

## **Fluid Visions**

In a puddle, I see my shoes,
These reflections give me the blues.
A splash here, a splash there,
Who knew rain could cause such flair?

A frog leaps in with a grand display,
While I just watch, trying to play.
I'll be the king of this tiny dome,
But where's the throne? I want to roam!

Funny faces stare back at me,
With silly grins, oh how they'll be.
I'll throw a wink, they'll laugh and roar,
This watery stage, the perfect floor!

So let me jest with each drop that falls,
In this mirror world, eccentric calls.
We'll dance with joy, in our quirky scene,
This playful realm, forever keen!

## The Dance of Shadows

In the corner, they start to twist,
A shadow dance, you can't resist.
Whispers giggle as shapes align,
Suddenly, I'm doing the moonshine!

A cardboard cutout steals the show,
How did my sock puppet learn to flow?
With wobbly arms and a cheeky grin,
Together we'll jive, let the fun begin!

Oh, shadows waltz with lopsided glee,
Their silly moves are just for me.
I trip and tumble, what a delight,
In this dark ballet, we own the night!

So grab your friend, let's spin around,
In our shadow play, laughter's found.
We'll create a scene, all blindfolded bliss,
Chasing twilight, with a slapstick twist!

## **Radiant Encounters**

In the sun, my shadow does play,
It's got moves that no one can sway.
It moonwalks softly, as I do a jig,
A dance of light that's rather big!

A flicker here, a shimmer there,
My hair's a mess! What a wild affair.
The sunlight mugs, it takes a snap,
Of my strange pose, caught in a trap!

Bouncing beams make me squint and blink,
As I try to figure out what I think.
My brain shines bright, then takes a fall,
I end up laughing, that's all, folks, all!

These glimmers laugh as they pass by,
I wave hello with a silly sigh.
In this bright world, laughter ignites,
Radiant moments, oh, what delights!

## **Waves of Introspection**

At the beach, I ponder my fate,
While a crab sidles up, looking great.
It dances up, then scurries down,
With its tiny moves, it steals the crown!

The ocean giggles, a tickle on toes,
As I get splashed, everyone knows.
I tumble back, like a novice fool,
Surf's up high, but I'm in a pool!

A seagull caws, it joins the fun,
Pretending I'm a clever pun.
With sand in my hair, it's quite the show,
Waves of laughter, it's time to go!

So here I sit, a beach bum in glee,
With crabs and waves, wild and free.
In the chaos, I find my bliss,
In every splash, there's joy in this!

# Flowing Thoughts

In a world where thoughts collide,
I trip over ideas, oh what a ride!
My brain's a circus, a merry-go-round,
With tigers on tricycles, joyfully abound.

Each whim that pops makes me laugh and sway,
Like juggling watermelons on a sunny day.
With a wink and a grin, I bounce off the wall,
For sanity's boring; why not have a ball?

I ponder my breakfast, a rubbery egg,
Did I just fry thoughts or a dance on a leg?
Life's a funhouse, mirrors twist my plea,
Every reflection just tickles me free.

So come take a spin on my thought-streaming ride,
Where giggles and nonsense always collide.
In this merry mayhem, let joy be your guide,
For thoughts are just bubbles that bounce, slide, and glide!

## Circles of Serenity

Oh look, there's a donut, it calls my name,
A circle of sweetness in the reflection game.
I dip it in coffee, the breakfast of dreams,
As giggles erupt with marshmallow screams.

In circles we dance, our feet all a-twirl,
Spinning like tops, watch our hair unfurl.
A waddle, a jig, we unleash the fun,
As pigeons on scooters bask in the sun.

We laugh at the chaos, a buffet of glee,
Life's funny like chickens who wish they were free.
In circles we gather, no frowns allowed,
Just joy on our plates, and silliness proud.

So twirl 'round the park, let your laughter resound,
Collecting the smiles, they're gold to be found.
In whimsical rings, let your spirits ignite,
For happiness dances, oh what a delight!

## The Loop of Existence

In the loop of existence, I trip on my shoe,
Around and around, I just can't break through.
I squeeze through the door, only to be caught,
In a loop of my antics, I need a new plot!

I try to escape, but the cat's on my feet,
Its purrs are my handcuffs; oh, isn't it sweet?
I whirl like a top, my belly's in knots,
Life's just a funny mix of all that we've got.

I swirled with the coffee, danced with a spoon,
A wobbly moonbeam made me howl at noon.
What's real and what's fake in this loop so absurd?
I can't find the pause button; isn't that hard?

So let's twirl together, make hijinks our creed,
In circles of laughter, there's never a need.
With every loop spun, a chuckle awaits,
In the dance of existence, we'll tease all the fates!

## **Watercolor Reflections**

Splashing colors on paper, oh what a sight,
Swirls of my mishaps, they drift with delight.
My thoughts flow like rivers, a rainbow in bloom,
While doodles of ducks make my worries consume.

A brushstroke of laughter, a giggle, a snort,
In the sea of my mind, I swim and cavort.
I paint all the blunders in shades oh-so-bright,
For who needs perfection when chaos takes flight?

With every new splash, my doubts disappear,
Like polka-dots popping, there's nary a fear.
Life's but a canvas, we're all brush-wielding fools,
Creating warm sunsets instead of cold rules.

So dip into colors, let humor ignite,
We'll swirl in the mess and dance through the night.
In watercolor worlds where laughter's the theme,
Every stroke's a reminder to dream and to beam!

www.ingramcontent.com/pod-product-compliance
Lightning Source LLC
Chambersburg PA
CBHW062108280426
43661CB00086B/344